Simply Homeschool

2nd Edition Completely Revised, Expanded, and Updated

Have Less Fluff and Bear More Fruit

in Your Homeschool

by Karen DeBeus

Please visit me at www.simplylivingforhim.com and join me as we encourage each other to live more simply for the glory of God.

Acknowledgements

My first and foremost thanks goes to my Lord and Savior Jesus Christ, *who brought me out of the pit of mud and mire and set my feet on a rock! (Psalm 40) Without Him I am nothing, and with Him the possibilities are endless. (John 15:5, Matthew 19:26)*

It is my prayer to do everything for His Glory. Less of me, and more of Him.

I also want to thank my amazing husband and love of my life, my four beautiful children who have exceeded my dreams beyond my wildest imagination, and my parents, sister, and in laws who love me no matter what and accept me for who I am, and who I have become on this journey. And finally, all of those in the amazing homeschooling community out there whose love and support these past several years are much appreciated.

Preface

In a world that screams more, I want less. In a world that screams ME, I want You. In a world that is getting louder and louder everyday, I want to be still in the quiet. In a world that is getting faster each day, I want to slow down…and simply live...for Him.

I have always been a Little House on the Prairie girl at heart….longing for the simpler days of long ago. Truth is, life wasn't easy back then. It probably was just as complicated, but in a different way. Yet, there is something about that life, that has always appealed to me. People weren't as focused on themselves, since they needed to work together for survival. People had less materially, but they seemed to have more spirit. There is just something about it…

My heart yearns for that simple spirit. To be so focused on my Lord, that the stuff of this world has less and less value. To be so fixed on Him, that the things around me are the "extras" in life, not the "must haves." He is the only "must have."

What if we only lived with just enough?

What if we lived with only what we really needed?

For the past several years I have been writing at my blog, Simply Living for Him…about my journey to simplify all areas of my life- from my home, to my homeschool, to the mental clutter that can invade our minds in an information laden world. These ideas resonate with people because deep down our souls yearn to be free- free from the clutter that surrounds us; free from the distractions and traps of this world; free to live as God intended us to live…for Him. The devil loves to distract us, and these days it is far too easy to let the distractions win….yet, I have resolved to simply live…for Him. Will you join me?

Simply Homeschool

Nine years ago, God called me to homeschool…and I didn't go willingly. In fact, I went kicking and screaming. Everything was against me. My parents. The world. Even some friends.

Mostly myself.

I didn't believe I could do it. Homeschooling was something for "other" people…they were more organized, more disciplined, more "spiritual." Those were the people you saw on TV, who had it all together, yet were considered a bit "weird" by most standards. Secretly though, I think I always admired those people. Their kids seemed to be so well behaved. There was something about their family lifestyle that appealed to me. Taking trips with your kids to learn things, hands on studies…the togetherness homeschooling provided was alluring. Yet, it wasn't "normal" by worldly standards. It was something most people thought was weird. (Yes, I really cared!) I cared what *everyone* thought. My friends, my family, even strangers…

But…

God was calling me… and He didn't want me to care what anyone thought …but HIM.

As hard as it was, I did make the decision to homeschool. I was scared to death, going against the grain, but God showed me each day something to reveal Himself. To show me that homeschooling *was* part of HIS plan, even if it was not part of mine. He showed me that I *had* made the right decision.

Over the years, God has been faithful. He has guided me and blessed our family in so many ways. This a journey I never expected to be on, but can't imagine myself anywhere else. He has made this journey worth it in so many ways.

I wrote Simply Homeschool, a small eBook, originally published in 2011. The response was amazing. So many people contacted me to tell me it was what they needed. They were drowning in the clutter of " homeschool life" and were yearning to simplify. Three years later it remains a best seller. I must say, looking back, I was not sure anyone would even read the book. Writing was a hobby, certainly not something I ever thought would turn into a ministry or work. I had no idea the book would be so successful and admittedly, I am a little embarrassed at the early writing style and lack of proofreading.

Yet, God uses it all. Since then so much more has even happened, so I knew it was time to update that book. I have learned so much on this journey, and I desire to share that with others as an encouragement and a testimony to what God does. I have had the opportunity to speak at numerous homeschool conventions and groups, and to share what God does when we submit to His will.

Now, I have taken the original Simply Homeschool and completely revised, expanded, and updated it. The same nuggets of encouragement are still there at the heart, but I am excited to share so much more. I have added chapters and bonus features at the end.

I have continued my quest for simplicity. I want to rid myself of things that distract from what is important. I want to rid my life of those things that can distract me from the Lord. I hope you will find it an encouragement too, as you seek Him above all.

Join me on my quest for simplicity as I focus on... Simply Living...For Him!

Chapter 1

What Does it Mean to Simplify?

"For where your treasure is, there will be your heart also."
Matthew 6:21

What Does Simplifying Truly Mean?

Simplifying is sort of a buzz word these days. People are longing for simple, but do they know what that really means? Does it mean we have to be minimalists and survive on only the basics? Does it mean we strip ourselves of all material comforts? Does it mean we can't buy things? What does it truly mean to simplify?

When I talk about simplifying, I am getting to the heart...it is not just about getting rid of clutter or having less stuff. That is just a small part of it. Actually, that is the result of it. **Simplifying is really about having more Jesus.** This world is begging for us to follow it, but I want to follow Him first. **Simplifying**

Matthew 6:21

For where your treasure is, there your heart will be also.

gets to the heart of our desires.

What is in our heart determines how we will live. Plain and simple- if we are seeking stuff, then we are not seeking Him. The truth is we actually gain so much more when we simplify. It is not really about having less, but more of what matters. We weed out the extras, the distractions, and the unnecessary stuff, in order to keep our eyes on the Lord. In return we see more clearly, we are more focused, and we even have more of ourselves to give to Him.

Years ago people lived with much less. I remember visiting an old farmhouse from the Revolutionary War on a family vacation. When I stepped into the farmhouse my attention was drawn to how little they had. There was just one or two rooms in the house to take care of, just enough pots and pans for cooking, and all the clothes for a family of six hung on simple hooks. There were maybe a few simple toys for the children. There was just enough to meet their needs. Since they had to spend so much time doing work just to survive, they really didn't have time for extras.

As I stood there my mind went to the present. Nowadays people have houses ten times the size, filled with stuff. Yet we don't have to spend so much time working to survive. So why are we overwhelmed all the time? Imagine we could meld the two things together- having all the modern convenience that we have today- a dishwasher, washing machine, modern kitchen, etc. yet we still had just enough. We would have so much time! We wouldn't be overwhelmed with taking care of huge houses, shopping endlessly for more clothes, toys, gadgets, etc. We wouldn't have to work to survive and yet we would have all we need. Why aren't we content with that? Why do we have things so much easier today, yet we are busier than ever, more stressed than ever, and I would even go as far to say, we are less content than ever.

Whether it is material items we crave, or information, or we are always filling up our time with endless activity, the heart of the issue is that we are seeking something outside of the Lord. The more we fill up on worldly things the less time and focus we have for God. He is the One who should fill us first. Where our treasure is, there will be our heart. He is our treasure. If we seek Him first, the Lord will provide all that we need. Most of the things we think we "need" these days, we really don't. They are merely extras. They may provide pleasure, but not lasting satisfaction. Our only true satisfaction in life will come from knowing the Lord Jesus.

People used to be more content with their lot. The more time goes on and the more people accumulate, the less content they seem to be. Think about it, we have it all in this country, yet we are a country that suffers from discontentment. Why is that?

I have known many people to travel to third world countries and they always say the same thing. The people they meet are the happiest people they have been with. Yes, the ones living in huts, or shacks with dirt floors. The children that are orphans even have joy. It is astounding, but they all say the same thing. They have so much joy in the Lord. When stripped of all the externals and there is nothing to boast in but the Lord, they are joyful. Their circumstances are not easy, they don't live in luxury...yet their external circumstances do not define their joy. Their joy comes from within. Their joy comes from the only thing that can not be taken from them. The Lord.

I crave that joy. I want that joy...do you?

All of our outside stuff really says so much about what is going on inside of us. True joy can only come from Him. Yet the more we buy, the more we toil, and the more we run about from one activity to the next. This says so much about our heart. If our heart is content in Him, the rest is really just extra. Unfortunately for many it becomes a burden- a burden of always wanting something more.

The truth is we can never have enough earthly things to satisfy us because we are not made for this earth. The only true satisfaction comes from above. In a great paradox, the more we have, the less content we seem to be.

On the other hand, we can have abundance materially and still be content, if our priorities are right. If we are truly content with the Lord first, and only Him, then of course there is nothing wrong with enjoying the blessings and provisions He gives us. However, I seem to wonder if we would still crave so much if we were truly satisfied with Him alone.

Overabundance

Perhaps overabundance has made us feel even more empty. Perhaps being surrounded by so much excess just makes us crave it more. Perhaps we are suffering from material obesity. The more we have access to, the more we want. The more we have, creates a desire to obtain even more. And we are never full. We are left empty.

Yet, if we were to strip ourselves bare of every extra, at the core we have Jesus. Yet, we have unintentionally buried Him down beneath all of the excess. We weren't content with Him and we craved the world, and before we knew it, we were looking to fill a void that had already been filled.

Does that make you cringe? It should. The God who created this world, who created you and me, who spoke the world into existence- and if that wasn't enough- chose us to be His, to be redeemed from the pit we were headed for, and then sacrificed His Son for us... that wasn't enough for us? We want all that, plus lots of extra earthly pleasures.

I don't say all these things to guilt you. I don't say it to be condemning and judgmental. **I am as guilty as the next person.** I say these things because they need to be said. To point us back where all of us have gone off track. We are all guilty to some degree of not putting Him first. My desire is to point us back to Him and give Him glory for all He has done. There is no guilt or shame, because He can redeem it all.

If you know Jesus, then it is time to go back to your core and remember, that in the end He is all we truly have. Everything else on this earth will fade away, and can be taken away at any moment. Except Jesus. He can not be taken away. He is our eternity. Isn't that enough?

In order to be truly full, we need to truly grasp that truth and live like it. **Live like Jesus is all we need.** Understand that truth. Then the desire to fill up on worldly things will become less, because we know our true treasure is only in heaven.

We need to build from our core up. Jesus is our core. Be content with truly knowing that He is our most prized possession. He is the only thing we need. He is the One that will fill us for an eternity. All else is just dust.

Matthew 6:33

"But seek first his kingdom and his righteousness, and all these things will be given to you as well

This is my life verse. It is one that I constantly am reminding myself of each day. If

I truly am seeking Him first, He provides the rest for my life. If I seek anything else above Him,

I end up empty. But when I truly seek Him first, I can trust Him to provide what I need, yet not necessarily what I want. Then I can live in freedom to enjoy the extras.

God knows what we need and He will provide it. We often think our needs are material, but He is looking to make sure our spiritual needs are met first. Those are the most important needs we have. The rest will fall into place only after those things have been supplied.

So where does one start to simplify? By stripping themselves bare of every worldly possession? Not necessarily. I think the heart of the matter comes down to reevaluating your true belief of the fact that Jesus is all you need, and then focusing on your spiritual needs first. It's a matter of trust. Trusting Him to provide all you need both spiritually and physically. And then walking in it. It's time to stop speaking it, but truly living it.

We need to be seeking the spiritual before the material. Those needs are the ones that last. Only then can we enjoy an material blessings He provides.

If that means stripping yourself bare of all else, so be it. For most of us though, I believe the desire to have more will lessen once we walk in the truth that Jesus is all we need. For years I have always felt out of place in many ways. As a child I believe it was labeled, "underachiever." I always sort of looked a things in an eternal perspective, "How much does this really matter in the grand scheme of things?" And as I have come to understand more about my desire to simplify, I have realized, it is not necessarily being an underachiever, but truly knowing what to weed out in this world. Eternal perspective matters.

Chapter 2

Simply Homeschool

"But seek first his kingdom and his righteousness, and all these things will be given to you as well."
Matthew 6:33

Simply Homeschool

Applying the principles of simplifying naturally permeate into my homeschool. This is the place God teaches us so much, and He uses homeschooling as a tool for us to glorify Himself and to minister to our children. However, the homeschool movement has grown so much in the past decade. It has exploded with resources and information causing some of us to feel distracted, disheartened, defeated, or even lost.

As a homeschooler just starting out, I really did appreciate all of the available help that was out there. However, as most of us do-we fall into the trap of getting sucked in to all of the information out there, and it is like we are constantly chasing our tail.

**We are constantly trying to do things better
or worse like someone else.**

I want to tell you to stop. Slow down. Stop chasing. Stop striving. Stop making about it about the world. Make it about Him. This world and all it has passes away, but He is eternal.

Stop. Look in your child's eyes. Focus on the relationship with the child. At that moment. These are the things that matter for eternity.

Let the extras go...if they are bogging you down, then they aren't meant to be there. This journey isn't going to last forever. In fact, each year it gets shorter and shorter...so do it well.

I always tell my kids to do all tasks well. Whatever lies before them, no matter how big or small, do it well. So, we as homeschool moms...are we doing it well? Are you stretched so thin we are giving a little in a lot of places? Or are we focused on what really matters?

When I first started homeschooling, I had no idea the amount of information available to homeschoolers and all of the resources that were out there. I was so excited to dive right into it all and learn all I could. Yet as time went on, I became one that was always planning and not doing. I was always searching for the next best thing in curriculum, methods, projects, etc. I spent so much time looking at everything out there, I was forgetting to focus on homeschooling itself. And most of all on why I was doing it…FOR HIM. I was so focused on doing it "right" I was forgetting what my main goals were- to disciple my children. Homeschooling is about so much more than academics.

Simplifying is about putting God first in EVERYTHING, including our homeschools.

Matthew 6:33

"But seek first his kingdom and his righteousness, and all these things will be given to you as well."

I saw that happening. When I sought Him first in everything, including our homeschool, He provided. I saw that when I obeyed the call God had given me to homeschool, He blessed us. Even when I was scared to death, even when it was hard, if I put Him first, He was always faithful. He has continued to work in ways I never dreamed possible.

However, many times, I also saw the other side of it. The times where I tried to do it in my own strength, or I put the things that didn't really matter first. I wanted the perfect "homeschool room," or the perfect curriculum with children who obeyed all the time. I ended up feeling defeated and ready to throw in the towel. I couldn't remember the big picture and why I was homeschooling. Thankfully, the Lord always reminds me, and through so many lessons, I have learned what I need to do when it gets rough.

So, take a moment to think back to why you decided to homeschool. Was it because you wanted more family time? Or you were unimpressed with public schools? Did you want to provide a biblical foundation for your child?

Whatever the initial reason you decided to homeschool was, always remember the most important one is **because God called you to**

homeschool. Ultimately, you would not be on this journey, if God had not put you here and He has a purpose for it all. He called you here.

The idea that I should homeschool started with a nudging. A pulling. A tug. Ok, then it was a full force dragging me to do it! It was a decision I prayed and prayed over, and was met with much resistance; from family, from friends, and definitely from myself. Yet the Lord kept showing up.

Everywhere I went I would be bombarded with things pertaining to homeschool. I would see an article about homeschooling, bump into a homeschooler- it was chasing me down! So I obeyed the call. It wasn't easy, but I did. It is the one time in my life I can say with full assurance, I fully trusted God, and boy has He blessed us.

Let me tell you a little story about how God provides in the most unexpected ways:

It was the eve of the day we would start homeschooling for the very first time. My daughter was beginning kindergarten, and all of her preschool friends were starting in their own schools. Most of them were in public school. As each friend would talk about preparing for the "first day of school" I started to doubt myself. Was my daughter missing out? She wasn't having her first day. Was this crazy idea really from the Lord? Maybe I was making a mistake.

I spent an evening in agonizing prayer. The kind where you just cry out to God and feel like He is not answering and you are lost. I felt lonely and scared. I couldn't even talk to my husband because I just wasn't ready to verbalize my fears.

I grabbed my Bible and started searching aimlessly for verses to comfort me. I was randomly searching pages, and nothing at all spoke to me. I was literally asking Him to show me a verse to say it would be OK. I truly felt helpless.

My family had been against my decision. I was upset that they were upset with me and our relationship would suffer because of this. I was so distraught.

Then at about 10 pm, the phone rang and it was my sister. It wasn't normal for her to call me, let alone at that hour. It turned out she had a question to ask me, which I can't even remember anymore what it was, but we ended up chatting for a bit. We hadn't talked much about my decision to homeschool previously, and I knew most of my family was not happy about it. Then toward to end of the conversation she said to me,

"By the way, I was in the grocery store tonight and the cashier asked me if I was preparing for the first day of school. I told her yes and asked her if she was doing the same. She answered me by saying no, because she homeschooled her children. I then told her that my sister was starting out homeschooling and she told me, 'You tell your sister she is doing the right thing. It is the best decision I have ever made. Let your sister know she is doing the right thing."

I nearly dropped the phone. Here was my sister telling me a story about a conversation in the grocery store and God used that cashier to minister to me. Unexpected? YES. Unbelievable? YES. Isn't God amazing?

After that reminder I felt incredible peace. I was sure that everything would be OK and it was. Nine years later, I can truly say I made the right decision. I followed God's calling and He has blessed us in so many ways.

Ephesians 3:20

"Now to him who is able to do immeasurably more than all we ask or imagine, according to his power that is at work within us"

When we put God first in our homeschool, He blesses our endeavors. We need to keep our eyes on Him and remember why we are homeschooling in the first place. We can't forget about why He called us, and that our mission field is our children.

I want to remind you that when the homeschooling movement began many years ago, there were no big fancy curricula, no homeschool conventions, no co-ops, and for many there weren't even others in their circle that homeschooled. It was a lonely place I am sure for many. A scary place. yet, those pioneer homeschoolers had their convictions and they had their God. I bet they had to fully rely on God and prayer to get through. They didn't have all of the resources we have today, and because of them we are here today. God works. Abundantly. They are living proof that we don't need all of the extras if we are truly relying on God.

So take a minute to **write down how you felt** in your initial years of homeschooling, whether it was this year or ten years ago. Write down why you started to homeschool. Then, **write a family mission statement.** What are your goals for your family? {*Not for anyone else's family but yours...*} Refer to it often. Better yet, post it around the house, so it's a constant reminder. As a homeschooling family you will have some days that are not so great. You will need to be reminded.

Always remember why God called you here.

I would encourage you to keep a journal as well. I can't tell you enough how this has helped me. As humans, we are so quick to forget. We can easily forget what God has done in the past. I have read through my journal that I wrote that first year of homeschooling, and it is an amazing testimony to what God has done. I see the prayers I wrote, the desperate feelings I was having, and the fears that plagued me. Now in the present, I can see how God has worked through all of that. It is clearly all His doing. Keeping a journal is not about necessarily what it will do for you in the present, but more importantly for your future self.

So I encourage you to write down your prayers, your fears, and your goals. Let God work through it, and then look back and see...He is faithful.

It is truly amazing to see that most of the blessings that God has bestowed on us during this journey are not at all the things I thought they would be. I have been surprised many times that most of the lessons learned on this journey have nothing to do with academics. He has brought our family closer to Him through this journey. The most important lessons have rarely come from textbooks.

Chapter 3

Reduce Physical and Mental Clutter

"But store up for yourselves treasures in heaven, where
moth and rust do not destroy, and where thieves
do not break in and steal. For where your treasure is,
there your heart will be also."
Matthew 6:20-21

Finally, brothers, whatever is true, whatever is noble,
whatever is right, whatever is pure, whatever is lovely,
whatever is admirable — if anything is excellent or
praiseworthy — think about such things.
Philippians 4:8

Reduce Physical Clutter and Mental Clutter

Physical Clutter

Remember that 18th century farming family? They didn't have much clutter to fill up their time, but they had lots of work. They all had chores that were things they needed to do *in order to survive.* We don't have to do nearly as much labor in order to survive these days, but we have filled our time with other things. One of these things being material items.

Physical clutter is all of the piles of **stuff** that fill up our homes. As homeschoolers we are unique because we work in our homes- all day, everyday. Not only does that make more clutter, but we are constantly distracted by stuff in our homes.

It boggles my mind that we have television shows devoted to helping people get rid of stuff and organize stuff. We have Pinterest boards and blog posts all about managing our "stuff." We have books lining our shelves all telling us how to handle all of our messes. We have storage units filled to the brim because our homes have run out of space. There is so much poverty in the world and here we are devoting TV shows that portray people who are "suffering" in their "stuff." It's just too much.

We need to stop collecting things and start doing things. Fruitful things. All of this "stuff" does affect our homeschools. I have seen it firsthand.

Un-cluttering Our Day

I remember one day I was working on math with my son. He was doing well so I decided to leave him be for a bit to work independently. I figured I would sort through some clothes that had been sitting in piles in our living room- hand me downs from another church family. So I started going through the piles and sorting them. Then I headed down to the laundry room to bring some of those piles to be washed, and on my way, stopped in the kitchen to drop off some clean dish towels. While in there I realized I had no plans yet for dinner, so I opened the fridge. Seeing I was out of milk, I decided to go back to the office to add it to my list... {*sound familiar?*}

When I walked into the office there was my son staring into space, math problems still undone. "What are you doing there just staring into space? Why aren't you doing your math?"

"I'm waiting for YOU."

{Gulp}

We've all been there. It's hard. We are trying to run our homes, be the mom, be the teacher, be the wife, be the maid, etc. We have so much on our plates! So the less we can take off of our plates, the better. One way to do that is to eliminate piles of stuff.

Books

In a homeschool, books are one of our best resources, but they also take up the most room. We love having our bookshelves lined with educational materials. Yet we need to be selective. Choose the books you must own~the classics, some dictionaries, reference books, best loved treasure, etc.

I love the real thing-really I do. But there is also a place for eBooks {*wink wink*} and books on Kindle or another e-reader. I believe having a good mix is great. Ebooks help eliminate clutter and can help by just printing out what you need. Kindles and other e-readers can eliminate clutter in an obvious way. So choose wisely. Plus, with e-readers you can take lots of books with you on the go!

So take some time to go through your bookshelves. Are the materials worth holding onto? Will they really be read again? Or are they just taking up space in case one day you might read it again? Do you really just like the "look" of having so many books to impress others? Are they necessary to hang onto for resources later on? Are there too many "fluff" books? Choose the best ones. Give the rest away.

Supplies

We all want a well-stocked craft area, school supplies, etc. Yet not all of us have the rooms in our homes to accommodate such things. Again choose what is necessary. Pens and pencils, special art supplies, etc.

Do we need four world maps? Do we need seven sets of flash cards? Do we need every educational board game there is?

At one time when people found out I homeschooled, they would give us lots of these items. I was incredibly grateful. Yet as time passes we really need to take an inventory of what is really beneficial to hang onto and what we can do without.

Scale down on the items you have. I promise you, you will not regret it. The less physical stuff to manage, the more time to spend doing things that are meaningful.

Most importantly, when it comes to supplies everything must have a home! And everything must return to its home at the end of the day!

I use this analogy with my kids:

When we eat dinner, afterwards we put the dishes into the dishwasher .

When they are clean, we take them out of the dishwasher and put

them back into the cupboard. Do we leave the plates wherever we feel like

it?

{On the couch, under the couch, on the floor?}

NO. So why is it different with anything else? If you use a supply, toy, etc.

it goes back where it belongs!

(note- this is still a work in progress ;)

And teach this as young as possible. It's much harder to train an older child on this, than one who has been doing it all along. And of course, modeling it yourself is the best way to teach our children.

As homeschooling moms we want the best for our children. We want to give them all that is offered out there. But when we fill up our homes with so much stuff, we are doing just that. **Filling up.** Then we need to constantly organize, and we find we are just moving piles around.

Make a list of the things that are absolutely essential. For example core curriculum books, supplies, etc. Then look around and see what is just fluff-those extra maps, flashcards, games, puzzles {with missing pieces}, etc. Decide what is necessary. Then look around and see what is just taking up space. We don't realize it, but that stuff weighs us down. Once we get rid of it, we feel so much freer!

Everyone works better in a less cluttered environment. And when there is less to take care of, it is easier to stay organized.

**When we spend more time trying to find
ways to organize our
stuff, and to make it look pretty while
organizing it, than on
actually using it, that is a red flag.**

We seriously spend a great deal of time on
"organizing" these days. The internet is full of
ideas on how to stay organized. I think that is a
symptom right there of too much stuff. We
spend more time trying to find the perfect
system of keeping track of our "stuff" than on
actual fruitful activities. We try to find ways to
make all of our stuff look "pretty." It's time
wasted that is not fruit bearing. Scale down.
Keep it simple. We shouldn't need an elaborate
system to organize our clutter. If it is stressing
you out, then it is time to let it go.

Mental/Spiritual Clutter

I found as I started on my homeschool
journey, I was always learning/planning, and
not actually doing. Everything looked so good, I
kept switching things. I would make elaborate

plans, and then see something else that looked good and get distracted.

Internet info-blogs, websites, facebook, etc. are full of so much valuable information, but you must learn to set aside time specifically for it. Otherwise you get sucked in and waste time. And you must scan only what articles are necessary-so much of it is good, and you get sucked in and end up filling your mind with too much. It is information overload.

I love the online community as a homeschooler. I love being able to connect with other adults during the day! For me, reading facebook, blogs, etc. is my social life during the day. I get to connect with adults! Yet, it is much too easy to start reading things, start doubting yourself, and getting mentally cluttered.

We spend time reading books on "how to" do things when it takes away from time in the WORD. When it comes down to it, the most important thing we need to read is the B-I-B-LE! God will supply all of our needs. We must turn to Him first!

Philippians 4:8

"Finally, brethren, whatever is true, whatever is honorable, whatever is right, whatever is pure, whatever is lovely, whatever is of good repute, if there is any excellence and if anything worthy of praise, dwell on these things"

So now the rule is, Bible first, extras come second. At one time, I took a break from facebook and internet articles. I felt like during the day if I needed to connect with someone, I could go to my Bible. I could connect with GOD at anytime. It was awesome. I felt like He was saying, "I've been right here all along… waiting to supply all you need." Connecting with Him first is essential.

Since then, I have gone back on the internet again, but with moderation and with the caveat that if I find myself there more than the Word, it is a problem. I want to fill my mind with HIM first. Yet, I am constantly evaluating the us of my time, and what I fill my mind with. As soon as I feel empty inside or like my mind is on overload, I know it is time to take a break. Keep yourself accountable- write down the actual time spent online. You will be surprised at how much time adds up. We say we don't have "time" for so many things, but if we cut out the extras, I bet we would have plenty of time that we didn't realize we were wasting.

I want my kids to look back some day and see that mommy was a praying mommy. A mom who was always in the Word. I want them to remember me on my knees, with a Bible at my side always. I don't want them to look back and remember mommy being in front of the computer all of the time or in front of the TV. Or filling the house with needless stuff from another shopping excursion. I want them to see that God was the most important thing in my life. That is a huge lesson for them, and is bigger than any lesson in a school book.

Technology is a friend and a foe. Oh, how I love the internet and the online communities I am involved in. Oh, how I also loathe it at the

very same time. It is yet a other tool in the evil
one's box to distract us, give us a false feeling of
security, and time waster. Not to mention, it
truly fills us up on too many extras, and not on
His Word.

Imagine we spent the equivalent amount of
time praying that we do online chatting? Or if
we were in the Word the same amount of time
we research online? We would be so filled up
with wisdom we wouldn't desire the endless
amounts of useless information we fill our
minds up with. Choose God over Google every
time!

The internet has made our world bigger-
and smaller- at the same time. All of a sudden
all the information we want is available to us at
any moment, Yet, how can our minds possibly
wrap around this. The results is we find
ourselves scrolling, staring, and aimlessly filling
up on information that leaves us feeling emptier
than before.

Online time also ups the ante these days on
the need for "stuff." Take one look at Pinterest

and you can easily feel inadequate.- like you need to have the perfect Pinterest party for your child with the perfect Pinterest cake. Again, Pinterest in and of itself is not bad; it is our distractible, covetous mind that is. We need to harness our control, take every thought obedient to Christ, and truly monitor our hearts while online. Are we truly looking for fruitful ideas or are we adding to our natural sinful desire to covet and want more?

Online time gives us a glimpse of another person's life. When we add up all of the "glimpses" we see of many people's lives, we get what looks like (falsely) the perfect life. It is a culmination of everyone's best, making us feel like we are living the worst. It is a trap and it is straight from the enemy. It is a distraction and it makes us covet even more.

Online time also eliminates the need for face to face relationships. We were created to be relational, and that means in real life, and not just over the computer. I am all for online support, but it can never take place of true intimate face to face relationships.

We need to look into people's eyes. Online relationships give us just one dimension. Real life relationships give us more dimensions. We need to be very careful to not get caught up in so much online time that we avoid real intimacy.

Don't Let Homeschool Become an Idol

Don't let homeschool become something that is bigger than HIM! Remember why you are homeschooling and keep your goals in mind always. You are homeschooling because God is using it as a tool for your family to grow closer to each other and to Him. Homeschooling is not the be-all-end-all, and it is not a guarantee that your children will turn out well. God needs to be first above all things, including our homeschool.

At one time, I started to let homeschooling become my identity, and my thoughts were more toward what books we would use and what methods, than on what God's plans for our family were. It was slowly becoming bigger than it needed to be. Homeschooling is a way of life, but it is not our life. It does not define our identity. Jesus does.

Don't succumb to the comparison trap. Don't compare to what everyone else is doing. It is very easy to get caught up in how everyone else is doing things, or in how other people's homeschool rooms "look." Seriously, does it matter if we have cutesy bins all matching and color-coded? Or if they are from the dollar store? Are our kids going to learn more based on how things look?

People are so focused on how they look on the outside, but homeschooling is about focusing on the inside. training up our children in the Lord. We need their hearts. A sucessful homeschool is not based on an orderly room that looks like a classroom.

**God cares what your kids hearts look like, not what
your homeschool "looks like."**

As homeschool moms we must remember that we are glorifying God each and everyday. We are teaching our children about him. We are planting His Word in their hearts.

We have to remember with each day that it is about Him. Think about Martha and Mary. While Martha was so busy running around trying to get everything done, Mary was sitting at Jesus' feet. Listening.

**I would rather be with my children sitting at Jesus'
feet, that running around trying to be busy or
create the perfect "homeschool room."**

God has called us to raise our children and raise them up according to His Will. We can't forget that. I truly believe that if we put the Lord first in all we do in our homeschools, He will bless us. We may worry that we are not doing things just right, or that our kids aren't learning enough. If my children know the Lord first and foremost, I have done my job. The education will come. They will learn. They will be fine...if we put Him first.

Chapter 4

Simplifying Schedules

"Commit to the LORD whatever you do, and your plans will succeed." **Proverbs 16:3**

Simplify Schedules

When it comes to schedules, homeschoolers are notorious for wanting the perfect schedule. But there is no perfect schedule. Life is variable, and teaching our children how to handle events that may interfere with our plans is actually helpful to them in the long run.

However, having a general flow to the day is important. Kids thrive on the predictability. But keep it simple. You do not need to schedule in 15 minute increments and have rigid plan to keep things running smoothly.

I have had all types of schedules over the years. I went from planning out every 15 minutes of our day, to having no schedule. As always, what works best is a happy medium. We have a general flow to our day but we allow for life to interrupt us. Some people will work well on a more regimented schedule and others work well on a spontaneous day. I have found for us, that middle ground always wins.

Start simple and avoid over-planning. You can always add more in, rather than feeling defeated by not getting it all done. Be flexible. Do not be a slave to a pre-printed out schedule.

Now remember- no schedule is perfect. And what works for me does not mean it will work for you. It is my goal to share our schedule so that you may glean from it what can work for you. Perhaps some ideas will work and some will not. **Pray over your schedule!** Again, let God lead your homeschool. Submit your plans to Him.

Remember your children are learning from the
time they wake up until they go to bed! Life is an education!

Our Typical Schedule {Sample}

We all usually wake up around 7am and have breakfast, do chores, hygiene, etc. At 9:30 am we start our school. I have been rigid with this time for a few reasons. One being, that kids, especially as they get older, need the discipline of being on time. No matter what time they wake up or if they haven't finished breakfast, chores, etc. we still start at 9:30. They must be ready.

At this time we then have Bible time together. **This is the most important part of our school day.** Again, putting God first is always the goal, so it only makes sense to start our day with Him first.

There was a time when I would skip Bible time if I thought we were having a busy day or we needed to get started. Until one day, I realized how ridiculous that was! How could I teach my children to put God first, if I was making math more important than God?

So now Bible time is non-negotiable. Since doing this, we have had very few days where I felt ready to throw in the towel. Starting the day with the Lord is a must.

A few years back we made this time even more important. We use this time for our family Bible study. We experimented with using the

Bible as our main textbook, meaning every lesson came from our Bible study. We realized how much science, history, language, and even some math was right there. It was an amazing experience. You can read about that in my FREE eBook Bible Based Homeschooling or visit my website www.Biblebasedhomeschooling.com. Since then we have added in other supplements, but we always begin with our Bible study. We have studied Genesis, Exodus, and the Gospels during this time. Each year we choose something else. We dig in deep using commentaries, concordances, etc. During this time we read the passage together and discus it. We pray together and then we sing worship songs or hymns. We often use YouTube to find the songs, so the kids can follow along with the words and the music.

This has become the new normal for us. There's no rushing to school buses, or rushing around to get out the door scrambling to find things. There's no kids all parting ways for the day.

No. For us a normal start to the day is when we are worshipping God as a family. And I'll tell you, this has given me my most special memories with the kids.

There is so amount of caffeine in the morning
that will wake me up more than seeing a two-year
with his hands in the air singing praises.

You can't help but have a good start to your day when you start it with Him. So we must make Bible time as a family a priority. Then we will be in the right frame of mind to start our homeschool day. Our hearts are all turned toward Him.

After Bible study we have our individual work time. Each child has a assignments to compete. We have used the workbox system over the years (many variations of it!) and now we just stick to mom giving assignments and getting them done. I have an older daughter now, so she works mostly all on her own. I work with the younger children as they need me.

When they were all little I divided up my time by age. The youngest would get me alone first. He needed me the most, so he would have his turn with me first. The rule was always, while I was working with any child during individual time, I was **not** to be interrupted. They were to work on their assignments and if they came across something they needed help with, they were to move on to the next assignment or wait quietly.

Once I was finished with the youngest, (about 30-45 minutes), I would move on to the next oldest. We would go over any assignments already completed while working independently, and then we would go over any new ones or things needing extra help.

Lastly, I worked with the oldest. By that time she had completed most work independently and we would go over anything she needed help with. This system worked well for many years.

Now as my children are getting older, I usually work on my blogs in the morning, and they work on their assignments. If they need help, they come to me. They know the rule about not interrupting if I am working with someone else, so they always wait until I am free. This took a few years of training, but I see the fruit.

We also have had toddlers/preschoolers in the mix over the years. I made very simple activity bags to be used during school time. They were just large ziplock bags filled with different activities. Examples are flashcards, homemade play dough, lacing cards, magnets, scissors and scrap paper, glue and scrap paper, trucks, sorting, etc. I changed these up so he didn't get bored of one activity. I also gave him worksheets to color and practice his letters and numbers. Preschool to me is never about "work" but about learning through play. They have always learned so much just by being around their older siblings. We include the preschoolers in anything they would like, but never "forced" them to sit. I let them set the pace.

After individual work is complete, it is usually lunchtime. We take a nice **long break** here. We prepare lunch together, and then have free time until 1pm, when we gather back together for together work.

This break was really important in simplifying schedules when the children were younger. First, for me, it gave me a certain time during the day that was **my time**. I knew during this time I could answer emails, make phone calls, throw the laundry in, start dinner preparations, etc. I knew each and every day I had that break so I didn't have to try and do things during school time. It really kept me focused. It was also really important for the kids to have this break. They knew each and every day they had this time to do as they pleased. Whether it was playing outside on the swing, playing on the computer, etc, it was their time.

Before we start back up with together work, we turn to the Lord. We always have had a **mid-day prayer time** where we pray for our time together and read scripture. Doing prayer again mid-day truly helps us refocus. If we have had a bad morning, bring it to the Lord in prayer. If things are going smoothly, thank Him for it. Focusing on Him in the middle of the day is a must.

Together work consists of Science, History, Geography, Artist study, Composer Study, and Nature study. We also use afternoons as less formal extensions of our formal work. The children are free to play in different areas I have created: Building areas, crafts, outdoors, etc.

Incorporating all children into as many subjects as possible is definitely a big part of simplifying homeschool. For grades K-5 this is easily done. Once middle school years hit, though, the older children did more individual studies.

These are the subjects that can simplify your schedule by doing them together:

Science

We have used Apologia products for years for Science and it works wonderfully. We all read the chapters aloud together and then do the experiments or hands on activities together. Then, each child has a notebook that you can purchase, and each one has either a "junior" book or the regular depending on their age. Here is where the older children can get more out of each lesson, and the younger ones can keep things on their level. I love Apologia for these reasons.

Science can also consist of many things not in a book- especially int he younger years. Nature walks, star gazing, kitchen experiments, etc. Read books about scientists. Use everyday life to point out science. Most of all talk about how our Creator is truly amazing in all He created. He is the author of science.

Science in the younger years really can consist of opening our children's eyes the world around them. Memorizing a bunch of science facts is not science. Discovering, exploring, and engaging in the world around us is. Let your children's natural curiosity lead them in this area. It doesn't have to be a complicated curriculum, but a natural discovery.

We have used our garden in the spring time to be our science lessons. From the planning of the garden, to the planting and harvesting, the children were involved. Each day we would measure the plants to see how much they had grown. We used a notebook for each child to record their observations. They helped pick put the plants, water, weed, and harvest. They were out there everyday working and observing. We learned so much about God's creation that year. We also used our notebooks to write out verses about plants and flowers, write poems about plants, and short stories. Language was incorporated right there in a very natural way. There was no formal textbook, but God supplied an ample amount of lessons.

History

We have used Truth Quest History with the Binder Builders, Beautiful Feet books, and Story of the World over the years. All of these worked well with multiple ages. For Truth

Quest, we simply read from the reading list. That included great historical fiction books, as well as some non-fiction. We have always been careful to select "living books" to eliminate fluff. We use all level books, so each child is exposed to many different things. Sometimes we will be "stuck" on a time period we love-for example, the Pilgrims. We have read every book we could about them because the kids were so interested. This is true learning. Other times, we may spend less time. I see no reason why we have to spend only a certain amount of time on each time period. True learning takes place when it means something! We don't necessarily follow a schedule for history.

When we used Truth Quest, once a week we worked on making our history binder, which helped reinforce what we had learned. We also would do some hands on things along the way to go with our lessons or watch some documentaries on Netflix.

We have also had years where we don't follow a "curriculum" for history at all, but just read lots of books on the time period. For instance when we studied Genesis, we read so many books from Answers in Genesis. We looked for historical fiction and non-fiction books and read them together. We learned about the Flood and Creation.

When we studied the gospels we read tons of books on Ancient Rome. We researched the time period to understand the Bible even more. We wanted to know exactly what life was like during the period we had been studying. History naturally was learned during our Bible studies.

We spent several years on American History when the children were young. We took field trips to Plymouth, Williamsburg, and Gettysburg. These were my favorite memories. After reading about these places, to actually see them in real life was amazing. True real life learning and living history at its finest.

Art

We usually pick an artist and study their artwork once a week. I would leave the artwork on display all week to make sure the kids were immersed in it. We would read books about the artist and mostly just enjoy their artwork .Simply Charlotte Mason has great resources for this! All the ages could be included in artist studies.

The purpose of these studies wasn't necessarily to memorize facts about an artist's life or style, but to be exposed to good art. We would keep notebooks about the artists, and then try to recreate our own artwork in their style.

Music

We would study a composer and listen to their pieces. Often we will listen in the car, in the background at home, and then more formally during a composer study. I would much rather have my children be exposed to the music, recognize various pieces, and appreciate the music, than to have them memorize facts about the composer's life.

Classical Kids CD's are great for learning composer study. As with art, we weren't as much interested in memorizing facts but in exposure to different styles of music.

Nature

Nature study is the most "natural" thing for a child. Children have the natural inclination to explore their surrounding when outdoors. Turning over rocks, studying bugs, identifying leaves, etc. are all natural learning and exploring.

At least once per week though, take sketchbooks outdoors and have the child pick one thing to sketch. There is a big difference in "seeing" a flower and "sketching" it. When they sketch it, they notice details. They notice things they would not just by seeing it. It becomes pictured in their mind.

Multiple Age Learning

I love incorporating the whole family in learning because it makes planning easier and promotes healthy relationships by working together. The best thing about homeschooling is seeing the children's relationships blooming in a natural way.

HOMEschool Means Being Home

Another area where homeschoolers are trying to fill up is outside activities. Deep down I wonder if this is because we feel a need to measure up to what everyone else is doing. It seems these days everyone is running around. The more scheduled activities, the better. The more classes, sports, and activities your child is signed up for the more "well-rounded" your child is. Ah! Let my child not be "well-rounded" then!

Kids need to be kids. Let their afternoons be filled with exploring {especially outdoors.} They need time to be by themselves, even if that means being bored sometimes. They need to have that down time to find what they enjoy doing, to actually be alone.

We do activities outside of the home, but we limit them. We have one full day where we are outside of the house for a fine arts program. There is another evening we are out for church activities. But the other days we really try to be home and focused on what we need to do at home.

I also find that the problem with outside activities is, as moms, we start to become so engrossed in the activity we end up overwhelmed. For instance, I've joked if you put my in charge of a program or a party at church, you better know it's going to be simple. I would rather have people using their energy and their time for the Lord in ways that mean something. The details often overshadow the truly meaningful things. I am all about not focusing on the details of what decor, what food, what extras do we want for a program...and all about what are we truly doing. What is the heart of the activity? Not the extra fluff.

I am always evaluating the use of my time. Saying no to activities is huge. My mantra is always, "in the grand scheme of things...does this matter." I have always been aware that my time here on earth is short (sometimes I must stop and remind myself) and I need to not get wrapped up in the small things, but keep my eyes on the big things. On eternity. Do I need to have my kids running around busy everyday, or do I want them siting at Jesus' feet, learning from Him. This world is a busy place and it is so easy to get caught up in it thinking, you "must" do this or that, when in reality, it may not be bearing fruit.

I find that as a people we like to be busy. Maybe we think busyness means success or fulfillment, yet often times it ends up making us emptier than before. Sure we may be filled up on stuff and expending tons of energy, but is it truly where we want to spending that energy and effort? I see this problem in churches, in homeschool groups, moms groups, or anywhere else that we "organize" groups. What happens is, the goal of the group or of the initial purpose gets lost in the stuff. We form homeschool co-ops so that we can help each other out with subjects, have some socialization for our kids, and we end up putting so much effort into the "group," we forget about why we started in the first place.

Groups grow and the next step is we have committees, councils, meetings, policies, etc. What went from a group that was supposed to provide a need, and ends up creating even more needs than when we started. Meetings, policies, and all the extras take so much time and energy. That very energy we can be putting into our own homes and our own families, ends up getting expended outside of our need. We say we are doing it in the name of serving, but who are we serving? Our first and foremost duty is to serve at home. When these outside duties distract us we end up stressed, short with our own kids, burnt out on all of the activities, meetings, and extras, and we don't have enough energy at home. Then we say that we are tired and burnt out on homeschooling, but really, if we put so much effort in at home, and less outside, that may not be the case.

I am not opposed to co-ops or any organized activities at all. I am just cautious of the need to enjoy being part of groups, and to be needed, which in turn ends up taking away from our own homes. I say this speaking from my own experience, not at all saying this is everyone's experience. Can you relate to the following?

When I first became a stay at home mom, I joined a local moms group. I had one child and it was a great place to meet other moms and children for my daughter. It got us out of the house and gave us opportunities to get involved with others. As time went on, I became more involved. I served on the board of the group and before long I became president. This meant monthly board meetings, newsletters, calendars, committees, and more. All in the name of having some friends? I realize looking back, precious time was lost with my little ones, while I was on the computer creating newsletters, writing meeting agendas, notes, reports, etc. All in the name of having friends for my kids? It became more about the group than the purpose that I intended when I first joined the group.

I saw the same thing with our family in church over the years. Serving on boards, committees, and groups meant meetings, reports, and lots of extras that took my focus away from my purpose at church which is to worship God and serve my community, in exchange for lots of extras. Yes, we need to organize groups and have policies, but I don't know that is what was intended in the early church. This is still something I pray about and think about often. Is this what God really wants in our churches?

These kinds of things can happen in any group -whether it is a homeschool group, a baseball league, girl scouts, etc. It becomes more about the group than the purpose. I long for simplifying these things, not getting caught up in the name of "serving" but just doing. It may mean limiting my time in such groups, or at least being very cautious into how involved I get.

~Being a homeschool mom is a full time responsibility-
I have to accept the hours from 9-3 are not my own, but belong to my children.
Although I receive no pay monetarily, the rewards are priceless and I feel truly rich~

Chapter 5

Simple Meal Planning

"While the earth remains, seedtime and harvest,
cold and heat,
summer and winter, day and night, shall not
cease."
Genesis 8:22

Simple Meal Planning

I believe meal planning is essential to simplifying homeschool and having smoother days. How many times does it end up being 4:00 pm and you are running around trying to figure out what to make for dinner? A little planning goes a long way in this area to keep things flowing smoothly. You can avoid the constant question of "What's for dinner" and the trap of serving chicken nuggets at the last minute with some simple strategies for planning ahead.

I make a 2-4 week meal plan. I keep a master list of all the meals we enjoy, along with recipes to try in my binder. When it is time to make my meal plan, I pull out the list for ideas. I also see if there are any new recipes I want to try.

Next I look at the calendar for the upcoming weeks. I plan easy meals on busy days. For instance, we are out of the house all day every Tuesday. So that day is always a crock-pot meal.

We come home at 4:30 and dinner is waiting for us. Perfect!

We also have days that are usually the same. Sundays are "Spaghetti Sunday." Now I may vary the pasta or the sauces, but it is almost always the same theme. So Sundays don't have to be planned.

Fridays are always homemade pizza. Again, I may vary the types but it is almost always the same theme. So, now I have Tuesdays, Fridays, and Sundays taken care of. Then I look at the other days and if I want to try a new recipe or make something more involved, I make it on a day where our schedule is light.

Using the calendar when planning meals is just so helpful. This way you can still try those recipes, but you do it when it is not overwhelming. And having days that are the same very week is so helpful in taking some of the planning "off your plate" so to speak.

Once I have my plan, I grocery shop for the ingredients needed. Now it is never perfect. Of course life gets in the way at times and we fall off the plan. But that's OK. We move on and try and stick with is as much possible.

Meal planning is really not as big of a task as people make it. Planning ahead is simply a way to maintain order and avoid stress when things get busy. Even a loosely planned meal is better than having nothing planned!

Chapter 6

Choosing Curriculum

And these words, which I command thee this day,
shall be
in thine heart: And thou shalt teach them
diligently unto thy
children, and shalt talk of them when thou sittest
in thine house,
and when thou walkest by the way, and when
thou liest down,
and when thou risest up.
Dueteronomy 6:5-7

Choosing Curriculum

Choose the curriculum that works for your family. Remember-for YOUR family. Not mine. Not your friend's. **YOURS.** God has a unique purpose for your family, and when you find something that works- stick with it. Don't get tempted to look elsewhere because someone else said it was good.

Homeschooling doesn't have to involve fancy curriculum and supplies. There is a world of information out there, and if we just utilize it properly, our kids can be educated just as well as any fancy curriculum. In fact, I bought one of those fancy all in one curriculums a few years ago. It truly is one of the best out there. I needed it that year because I was pregnant and figured I would let the curriculum do everything for me. However, now I choose not to buy one like that, but to gather different things from different sources. The library is really our best resource out there.

We have really **simplified** our curriculum. By simplifying though I do not mean lowering my standards, I just mean cutting out lots of fluff- focusing on what is important. **Our kids days don't have to look like the public/ private school's days.** They're not supposed to. *Our learning goes on from the moment we wake up until we go to bed.* And most of all, we are doing it all together...I see the kids interacting with each other and becoming so close.

Pray over your choices. Let God lead you. He placed you on this journey and He wants to lead you through it. Stick to His Word and pray without ceasing for your homeschool!

Don't always look for the next best thing. There will always be something better out there. If something is working well don't even open the catalogs. Stick with it and put all your effort into it. Don't get distracted!

I spent the first few years of my homeschooling switching from one program to the next. Now we have found a nice balance of different things. The things that work for us we stick to. I don't even entertain the catalogs in those areas. Once you find something that works, do get distracted by something else.

Simplifying homeschool also means rethinking our views on education. Remember our kids are learning to live independently in the real world some day, by living **in** the real world now. They're not hearing about things in classroom. They are living it.

Each day is a lesson whether a book is opened or not.

Your home can be the best tool in your curriculum. We teach real life skills, relationship building, stewardship, discipline, responsibility, etc. all just by living life and pointing out lessons along the way. Some of our best homeschool moments and most educational lessons have taken place spontaneously through real life. Always be on the lookout for life lessons!

Incorporate lots of extra activities to keep things fun. You don't have to make elaborate plans, but take advantage of local sites for field trips. We have loved learning history through lots of living history. We have visited many of the places we studied, and it is great to bring history alive. We have visited local planetariums when we studies astronomy. We visit local farms to observe the animals. There is so much out there to explore.

Special days can be very simple but also very memorable. For example, we have a tradition of working through all of the snowstorms in the winter time, even though the local schools get "snow days." My kids know that if we keep working on those days, when spring come and we get the first warm sunny day, we take off for a "sun day." We got to the park and have a picnic and take the day off! It is always something memorable! Create your own simple traditions that will be meaningful and bring your family closer together. It can be celebrating a special family day every year, or a "sun day" like us, or whatever you choose!

Unit studies are another fun way to change things up. A few years back we were studying

Colonial America. So in December we took the month to deviate from our "normal" schedule and did a Colonial Christmas Unit study. It was the perfect down time from our schedule since December tends to be a busy month.

Here are some practical ideas for natural learning:

- a day of research on a topic of the child's choice

- an afternoon spent listening to Mozart while painting

- a day in the yard observing an ant hill, a robin's next, or a bee hive

- a morning gardening, while learning all about compost,
  seeds, and zone planting

- writing creative stories, plays, or poetry

- a construction project in the home-complete with preliminary plans, blueprints, and the execution of the plan with the proper tools

• cooking up an authentic cultural feast after weeks spent reading about
  that country

• analyzing the nutritional content of your pantry

• grocery store math, while grocery shopping

• a day out to see a play or visit a local museum

• a visit to the local nursing home

• writing a letter to your sponsor child in Africa

• designing buildings on the computer

• helping with the finances by watching dad pay bills
  and budget (or do taxes!)

- chores, chores and more chores...all life skills!

- figuring out the how to build rockets, legos in 3D, and more

- raising chickens

- spending the day at work with dad as a mini-intern

- learning all about how day to day life works by being immersed
  in it and not a classroom!

Life is a classroom. Life is what we are preparing our children for. What better way to learn that with the hands on lesson of life?

I have found lately when I loosen the structure {not throw it away}, the kids are more free to pursue their interests and that is when they truly learn. When I don't see a separation between learning and life...they thrive...

And finally, we don't stress about doing "school at home." If I wanted my kids to be having the same education as the schools use, then they would be in school. But we use everyday opportunities to learn. We learn by doing. We learn by seeing. We learn by being immersed in life.

Chapter 7

What To Do With All That School Work?

Go to the ant, you sluggard! Consider her ways and be wise, which having no captain, overseer or ruler, provides her supplies in the summer, and gathers
her food in the harvest."
Proverbs 6:6-8

What To Do With All That School Work?

OK, so now that we have our curriculum and our schedules down, what do we do with all the schoolwork? Stuff piles up. Especially if you have a lot of little people creating a lot of stuff each day.

Depending on where you live, you will need to keep certain things for an end of the year review or portfolio. Where I live, I do not actually have to turn anything in. But here is what I do, for myself and to have something to show at the end of the year, just in case.

Each day, all completed work goes into a binder. The key here is **each day.** When I first started making a binder for completed work for each child, I would always set it aside for later. And by the end of the week I had huge piles and I would just "shove" it into the binder. {Not very neatly I may add.} The problem was the papers became too overwhelming and I just wanted it out of sight, so it got shoved away.

Now as soon as the paper is complete, it goes into the binder. We have the very large binders with a section each for Math, Language, Art, etc.

At the end of the school year I plan to have an "open house" for the grandparents to come and see all of the completed work from the year. We will highlight specific things, maybe do a drama, etc. It motivates me to keep things neat and orderly knowing I will be showing it at the end of the year.

Then when the whole year is complete, all used workbooks, the binders, any special crafts, projects, etc. go into a large plastic bin, labeled with the year. Then, into the attic it goes.

My Homeschool Binder

I also use a homeschool binder for all things related to our school for myself during the year.

Forms for outside activities

Lesson plans/planning sheets

Printouts for lessons/worksheets, articles, etc.

I have a section of the binder divided by weeks for the school year. I put the lesson planning sheets in for each week, and then I write them as we go along. I have a loose plan but I am always flexible to let life get in the way. I am too easily defeated if I plan ahead too much and we don't complete it all. So I keep it loose, and write the plans in a week or two at a time. Over the years I have used various planners, and sometimes just preprinted lesson plan sheets.

I also put into each week any worksheets to be used, or anything to "remind" me of something I want to use that week. I found I would often see things online to use, or eBooks to print, and then forget to actually use them. Now I print it out, and stick it into the binder so remember!

I also have a family binder where I keep all things central for the family. Product manuals, coupons, my meal lists, planning sheets, thank you notes, stamps, recipes to try, etc. Everything is in one place and I don't need to be constantly looking for items.

I would highly recommend taking the time to put these binders together. A little planning goes a long way later to stay organized and simplify stuff.

Chapter 8

Simply Preschool

Simply Preschool

Preschool is so simple. Really it is. It doesn't have to be complicated like so many make it. Want to know the best curriculum for preschool? Open your door and get outside. Explore nature. Explore your community. Talk to your preschooler. Explain things. Point out shapes,colors, number, and letters. Point to God is everything. Share the majesty of this world that He created.

A preschool age child is a sponge with a natural curiosity to learn. Do not squelch that by making him sit at a desk for a certain amount of time to do a worksheet. How stifling! Don't complicate things.

Little ones need to move and to explore. Take field trips. Visit parks. Visit museums. Most of all, enjoy these years together. There is plenty of time for book work in the next 12 years.

Sure, if you want to pull out some workbooks once in a while so your child feels like they are doing "school" like their big brother or sister, go for it. Yet, don't make that the only thing you do. Talk with your preschooler. Look them in the eye and engage in their questions. They will learn more from you at this time than a workbook.

But what about structure you may ask? Don't they need a strict schedule and a structure? Note necessarily. There can certainly be a flow to the day and a routine, but a regimented school structure is a bit much at this age. There are numerous studies out there that say when children spend their early years playing, they excel later on in academics.

Often times I will include our preschooler in any of our together work, but I do not "make" him sit through it. I realized over the years just how much a little one absorbs through being the room passively listening. I also will give them coloring pages just for fun, based on what we are studying. I have seen time and again how much they learn just by observing their siblings.

A preschool age child's schoolroom should be life. It is right there waiting for him to explore. **Here are some ideas for simple preschool:**

- A bean box- fill the bottom of a large plastic bin with dried beans. Let them scoop, dump, drive trucks or cars through it. It's like an indoor sandbox in the winter time ;)

- Scavenger Hunts. Indoor or outdoors, you can create just about any type. Learning shapes? Have them search for things that are specific shapes. You can also do this with colors, things that begin with a certain sound, or any lesson you want to teach. To make it even more exciting, I let my child take a camera along and take pictures of the things they find. (if you are comfortable letting your little one use your camera)

- Nature walks- always a hit with a little one. Bring a sketch book and let them draw what they see.

- Pretend play- let them be involved with what the big kids are learning. Have you older children act out something they are learning in history. Include the little ones. They will learn about history just by being involved in the skit.

- Field trips. Take advantage of your local museums, state parks, etc.

- Grocery store learning. Let your preschooler be involved in making the list, cutting the coupons, and shopping. Talk to them about budgets and nutrition. There are so many lessons right there!

- Practice writing letters and numbers with sidewalk chalk. Some of our favorite ways to learn numbers and letters were hopscotch games.

- Most all, talk, talk, and talk some more with your preschooler. Engage with them. They will learn from you each step of the way through life!

Chapter 9

Keep Your Eyes On Him And Press Ahead

"But one thing I do: Forgetting what is behind and
straining toward what is ahead, I press on toward the
goal to win the prize for which God has called me heavenward in Christ Jesus"

Philippians 3:13-14

Keep Your Eyes On Him And Press Ahead

Always remember that God called you to homeschool. He wants our children's hearts. He wants our hearts. We must keep our eyes on Him if we are to be successful in this journey. It is not about the stuff, but it is all about Him.

Homeschooling is hard, and we must lean on Him if we are to succeed on this journey. We must depend fully on Him. We need to let Him lead us.

Commit our homeschools to Him. Dedicate them to Him. He wants to lead us as we lead our children. Simplifying Homeschool is about getting back to the reasons that He called us, eliminating the distractions in our day that hinder us from keeping our eyes on those goals, and about living more simply, so that we may Simply Live…for Him!

It is important to fill up on Him before anything else each day. I have included at the end of this book 31 Days of Praying over your homeschool. You can print it out or use it as a guide to pray verses over your homeschool. He needs to be the first One we run to each morning. Nothing else can equip us like He can.

Remember on the rough days, that it is OK. God uses the rough times to help us. When things start to feel overwhelming, stop and evaluate. Are you getting bogged down with too much extras? Are you losing focus? Take a break and recharge. Keep your eyes on Him. Remember when Peter got out of the boat? He walked on water when His eyes were on Jesus. When he took them off of Jesus and looked at the storm, he sank. We will all have storms in life, so keep your eyes fixed on Him through each storm. Don't sink.

God wants to use our homeschools for so much more than academics. Allow Him to lead you through this journey. Let Him teach you as you teach your children. Thought this journey may be full of ups and downs, the rewards will be worth it.

1 John 2:16-17

For everything in the world-the lust of the flesh, the lust of the eyes, and the pride of life-comes not from the Father but from the world. The world and its desires pass away, but whoever does the will of God lives forever.

Psalm 37:5-7

Commit your way to the LORD; trust in him and he will do this: He will make your righteous reward shine like the dawn, your vindication like the noonday sun."

Bonus Features

*31 Days of Praying for Your Homeschool

*A Homeschool Mother's Prayer

*One Week Mom's Retreat- Plan and Prepare for Your Year

*Tips for Homeschooling Multiple Ages

31 Days Of Prayer for Your Homeschool While Seeking First His Righteousness

As homeschooling families, we must cover our homeschools in prayer. It is necessary if we are to succeed. If we seek Him first above all else in our homeschools, we will be on the right path.

Commit to using this guide for 31 days. Read one verse each day. Mediate on it. Pray over it, and see how it applies to homeschool. Read it as a family if you wish. Better yet, write it down somewhere prominent for the whole family to see. Let His Word penetrate the heart of your homeschoool.

We must seek His will diligently each day. Covering our homeschools in prayer will keep our hearts and our homeschools turned toward Him.

If you do this for 31 days, I am hopeful that it will become not just an act for those 31 days, but a lifelong commitment to praying for your homeschool.

As homeschool moms we need to fight off so many battles from the enemey-the world, and sometimes ourselves. Choose today to fight those battles with His Word.

Let God lead your homeschool. We rely never on our own strength, but solely on His.

Day 1
Matthew 6:33

But seek first his kingdom and his righteousness, and all these things will be given to you as well.

Day 2
Philippians 4:8

Finally, brethren, whatever is true, whatever is honorable, whatever is right, whatever is pure, whatever is lovely, whatever is of good repute, if there is any excellence and if anything worthy of praise, dwell on these things.

Day 3
Deuteronomy 6:6-8

These words, which I am commanding you today, shall be on your heart. You shall teach them diligently to your sons and shall talk of them when you sit in your house and when you walk by the way and when you lie down and when you rise up. You shall bind them as a sign on your hand and they shall be as frontals on your forehead. You shall write them on the doorposts of your house and on your gates.

Day 4
Isaiah 54:13

All your sons will be taught by the LORD, and great will be your children's peace.

Day 5
3 John 1:4

I have no greater joy than to hear that my children are walking in the truth.

Day 6
Proverbs 8:17

I love those who love me; And those who diligently seek me will find me.

Day 7
Hebrews 2:13

And again, I will put my trust in him. And again, Behold I and the children which God hath given me.

Day 8
Joshua 24:15

But if serving the LORD seems undesirable to you, then choose for yourselves this day whom you will serve, whether the gods your forefathers served beyond the **River, or the gods of the** *Amorites, in whose land you are living. But as for me and my household, we will serve the LORD.*

Day 9
Proverbs 31:15-17

She gets up while it is still dark; she provides food for her family and portions for her servant girls. She consid¬ers a field and buys it; out of her earnings she plants a vineyard. She sets about her work vigorously; her arms are strong for her tasks.

Day 10
Proverbs 22:6

Train up a child in the way he should go, Even when he is old he will not depart from it.

Day 11
Colossians 3:23

Whatever you do, do your work heartily, as for the Lord rather than for men.

Day 12
Matthew 11:28-29

Come to me, all who labor and are heavy laden, and I will give you rest. Take My yoke upon you, and learn of me; for I am gentle and humble in heart, and you will find rest for your souls.

Day 13
Proverbs 3:6

In all your ways submit to him, and he will make your paths straight.

Day 14
Proverbs 3:5

Trust in the LORD with all your heart and lean not on your own understanding;

Day 15
Matthew 6:19

Don't collect for yourselves treasures on earth, where moth and rust destroy and where thieves break in and steal. But collect for yourselves treasures in heaven, where neither moth nor rust destroys, and where thieves don't break in and steal. For where your treasure is, there your heart will be also.

Day 16
Psalm 40: 9-10

I proclaim your saving acts in the great assembly; I do not seal my lips, LORD, as you know.

I do not hide your righteousness in my heart; I speak of your faithfulness and your saving help.

I do not conceal your love and your faithfulness from the great assembly.

Day 17
Exodus 20:1-15

And God spoke all these words, saying, "I am the Lord your God, who brought you out of the land of Egypt, out of the house of slavery. You shall have no other gods before me. You shall not make for yourself a carved image, or any likeness of anything that is in heaven above, or that is in the earth beneath, or that is in the water under the earth. You shall not bow down to them or serve them, for I the Lord your God am a jealous God, visiting the iniquity of the fathers on the children to the third and the fourth generation of those who hate me, ...

Day 18

Romans 12:2

Do not conform any longer to the pattern of this world, but be transformed by the renewing of your mind. Then you will be able to test and approve what God's will is —His good, pleasing and perfect will.

Day 19

1 Corinthians 13:1-13

If I speak in the tongues of men and of angels, but have not love, I am a noisy gong or a clanging cymbal. And if I have prophetic powers, and understand all mysteries and all knowledge, and if I have all faith, so as to remove mountains, but have not love, I am nothing. If I give away all I have, and if I deliver up my body to be burned, but have not love, I gain nothing. Love is patient

and kind; love does not envy or boast; it is not arrogant
or rude. It does not insist on its own way; it is not
irritable or resentful;

Day 20
Psalm 34:17

When the righteous cry for help, the LORD hears and
delivers them out of all their troubles.

Day 21
Proverbs 23:12

Commit yourself to instruction; listen carefully to words
of knowledge.

Day 22
Philippians 4:13

I can do all things through him who strengthens me.

Day 23
Jeremiah 29:11

For I know the plans I have for you, declares the LORD,
plans for welfare and not for evil, to give you a future
and a hope.

Day 24
Galatians 5:22-23

But the fruit of the Spirit is love, joy, peace, forbearance, kindness, goodness, faithfulness, gentleness and self-control. Against such things there is no law.

Day 25
Ephesians 6:11-18

Finally, be strong in the Lord and in his mighty power. Put on the full armor of God, so that you can take your stand against the devil's schemes. For our struggle is not against flesh and blood, but against the rulers, against the authorities, against the powers of this dark world and against the spiritual forces of evil in the heavenly realms. Therefore put on the full armor of God, so that when the day of evil comes, you may be able to stand your ground, and after you have done everything, to stand. Stand firm then, with the belt of truth buckled around your waist, with the breastplate of righteousness in place, and with your feet fitted with the readiness that comes from the gospel of peace. In addition to all this, take up the shield of faith, with which you can extinguish all the flaming arrows of the evil one. Take the helmet of salvation and the sword of the Spirit, which is the word of God.

And pray in the Spirit on all occasions with all kinds of prayers and requests. With this in mind, be alert and always keep on praying for all the Lord's people.

Day 26
Psalm 119:66

Teach me good judgment and knowledge, for I believe in your commandments.

Day 27
Proverbs 9:9

Give instruction to a wise man, and he will be still wiser; teach a righteous man, and he will increase in learning.

Day 28
Philippians 4:19

And my God will supply every need of yours according to his riches in glory in Christ Jesus.

Day 29

Ephesians 3:20

Now to him who is able to do immeasurably more than all we ask or imagine, according to his power that is at work within us.

Day 30

Deuteronomy 31:6

Be strong and courageous. Do not fear or be in dread of them, for it is the LORD your God who goes with you. He will not leave you or forsake you.

Day 31

2 Corinthians 4:16-18

So we do not lose heart. Though our outer self is wasting away, our inner self is being renewed day by day. For this light momentary affliction is preparing for us an eternal weight of glory beyond all comparison, as we look not to the things that are seen but to the things that are unseen. For the things that are seen are transient, but the things that are unseen are eternal.

A Homeschool Mother's Prayer

Dear Lord,

May I teach them what you want them to know, and in turn You will teach me what You want me to know. Lord, let me remember my job is to point them to You, and not this world. Help me to guide them on the path that leads to You. Give me the strength when I feel I have none…When I don't feel like it, let me do it anyway. When I am tried, give me your divine energy to press on.

When I want to put myself first, let me remember Your words that I may be humble. Let me do this for your glory, and not mine. Lord show me each day the path we should take. When I get off course, thank You for Your mercy in bringing me back. Let me remember these children are Yours, and You love them even more than I do. Let me be thankful for the gift of spending each day with them. Let me remember it will be over in the blink of an eye. The complaining isn't forever, the noise isn't forever, the mess isn't forever...but You are.

And that is my goal...that we may spend eternity in Your presence. Let this homeschool glorify You, show You to those around us, and please You. Let me not get caught up in doing things the world's way, but Your way. Let me not be distracted by the noise of this world, from the true goals you have set.

Let me remember that the books are important, but Your Word is most important. May I see my children as the blessing they are that You created. Each unique and special with a purpose to fulfill.

May I remember how blessed I am to be a homeschool mom.

Amen.

One Week Homeschool Mom Retreat- Focus and Plan for Your Homeschool Year

Each year, before the beginning of your school year, set aside some time to prepare. This preparation should include spiritual needs as well as practical and physical needs. Set aside time each day to focus on a different area of your needs before the year begins.

Day 1

Pray

Use this day to focus on God. Seek His will for your family Forget what the internet, books, or even friends say are the "right" things to do." This is between you and the Lord. Spend time in prayer. Read the Word. Journal. Listen to Him. Worship Him. We are so good at talking to God, we often forget to sit at His feet and listen. Be still and seek His will for your family and for your homeschool.

Day 2

Write out goals

After you have spent time with the Lord seeking His will, spend a day writing out the goals for your family. These are unique goals that are unique to your family. Many of these goal will be academic, but don't forget the most important ones- the spiritual and character goals should be priorities.

Day 3

Evaluate your time/schedule

Pull out your planner and schedule in the necessities. Schedule a loose plan for your days. The "must-haves" should go first- math, reading, etc. Then schedule in the extra projects or crafts you would like to do. These are the things though that can get put aside if life gets in the way, or you have unexpected things. Schedule in outside activities. Remember, it is always better to schedule less and add more in than to begin the year overwhelmed. Schedule time for family prayer- one evening a week where the family can come together and talk about things more deeply and pray together. Schedule field trips, playdates, and mom retreat days during the year. Put them on the calendar now, or it may not happen when things are in full swing.

Day 4

Tackle mental clutter

When in doubt, turn to your Bible. Always choose the Word over Google. Then, only after you have searched God, seek out other resources. He will lead you to the right ones. Listen to His voice above all.

Evaluate your mental clutter how much time are you spending on articles, internet, books, etc. that are information overload? If necessary, keep a log of the amount of time you spend on the internet vs. how much time you spend in the Word. Adjust your time if necessary. Go through your resources and weed out those that are't bearing fruit.

Day 5
Tackle clutter

Once you have tackled mental clutter then you can tackle physical clutter. A clear mind works much better. Take an inventory of what is in your homeschool room and what you really need. Use simple organization to keep things tidy. Don't spend more time trying to make it "look" perfect than on function. Organize the books you will need for the school year and and put others away. During the year when things get slow or those cold winter months, pull out some fresh books. Your children will be more apt to look at them when hey are fresh and new.

Use simple bins for each child or a shelf. It doesn't have to be elaborate. Keep school supplies in an easily accessible place. Sometimes too much can be overwhelming.

Day 6
Meal plan

Take a day to plan meals for 2-4 weeks. This will make your days so much more smoother in the long run. It is worth the time to do it once. Use your calendar when planning so you can plan quick and messy meals for the busy day s (crockpots are great for busy days) and plan more involved meals when you a re home. Even better, enlist the help of older children on those days home and let them help in planning, prep, and serving of the meal. You will be teaching life skills at the same time. Meal planning also saves on the budget0- you can plan in advance what you need and not be left with extra grocery store trips for need times.

Day 7
Sabbath day

Take this day to pray again over all of your choices. Commit your plans to the Lord. Rest inHim and let Him lead you.

Tips for Homeschool Multiple Ages

One thing I have been asked many times by other moms is how do we homeschool multiple ages. I think the answer is much easier than you think. It it so much easier in the younger years to keep as many levels as you can together for certain subjects.

*Group as many as you can together-math and reading will be separate, but for grades k-6 you really can work together for science, history, arts, etc. Each child will go at their own pace, but learning the same themes.

*Let older ones do projects and age appropriate assignments while younger ones do things on their level

*Field trips- plan lots of good museums, state parks, or living history. All kids love field trips!

*Have older children teach younger children- the relationships that are formed are priceless when you let the children naturally mentor each other. Younger children learn to look up their older siblings and older children can reinforce what the know by teaching the younger siblings.

*Read all types of books to your children. You will be surprised how much the older children enjoy sitting through those picture books or classic stories. You will also be amazed at how much a younger child will gain just from sitting in the room and coloring while you read aloud a chapter book to the older children. Also, let your older children do the read alouds sometimes. This will help them practice reading out loud and the younger children will benefit from listening to their siblings.

*Assign a report on a topic of each child's choice. The older children can gather books and resources from the library and do a more formal report, while the younger children can find resources at their level. They can make a simple picture report. Have a day to invite grandparents or friends over and let all the ages present their topic.

*Have a spelling bee, geography bee, Bible bee, etc. for all ages. When my kids were younger we did "Fun Fridays" for this purpose. We used this day to do crafts or have game such as a Spelling bee. The older children would get words or questions for their level, and the younger ones could prance at their own level, but all ages participated together.

*Many curriculum out there is geared toward multiple ages learning together. Seek those out. Multiple ages learning to gather was incredibly beneficial when my children were younger in keeping things simple.

To read more about letting God lead your homeschool, check out my other books:

Called Home: Finding Joy in Letting God Lead Your Homeschool

Bible Based Homeschooling:
Our Experiment With Using the Bible as Our Main Textbook

Visit me at
Simply Living for Him
or
Bible Based Homeschooling

Made in the USA
Lexington, KY
25 June 2015